Journey to Financial Literacy
and Freedom

Journey to Financial Literacy and Freedom

Solomon Oppong
Felix Oppong Quayson

J. Kenkade
PUBLISHING®
Little Rock, Arkansas

Journey to Financial Literacy and Freedom
Copyright © 2021 by Solomon Oppong and Felix O. Quayson

J. Kenkade Publishing
6104 Forbing Rd
Little Rock, AR 72209

www.jkenkadepublishing.com

J. Kenkade Publishing is a registered trademark.

Printed in the United States of America
ISBN 978-1-955186-05-6

Dedication

We dedicate this book to our families and friends.

To those who are living a financially
distressed life.

To those who will like to learn more about
financial literacy and freedom when it comes
to personal financial planning.

Table of Contents

Acknowledgments

We'll like to acknowledge Kings Boachie-Mensah Jr., a teacher and educator in the Dallas Fort-Worth area in Texas, USA for his kind and special attention to details when reviewing the initial draft version of this book.

A special thanks to Dr. Felix Quayson for serving as Editor and Reviewer of this book.

To Our Families & Friends

Our primary goal with this book is to submit to you how to perform your financial management outlook including budgeting, saving, investing, and spending. Our secondary goal is to point you to valuable resources to help you along the pathway to your financial freedom by considering your level of financial risk and upcoming personal and professional future events.

CHAPTER 1
What is Personal Financial Plan?

"Financial peace isn't the acquisition of stuff.
It's learning to live on less than you make, so you
can give money back and have money to invest.
You can't win until you do this."
–Dave Ramsey

Living a debt-ridden (having too much debt and living financially a difficult life) and unnecessarily lavish lifestyle will always have its adverse effects on your finances. Financial planning is an umbrella term that covers a variety of pathways by diligently securing and planning your monetary resources, income, assets and liabilities evaluation, investments, savings and financial state of mind for the future. Whatever you do, always remember to pay yourself first. Take a portion of your income when you get paid and pay yourself by depositing the money into savings or investment funds.

According to a study published by Fortune in July 2016, nearly two-thirds of Americans can't pass a basic test of financial literacy. Hold on and read that again. The study surveyed 27,564 Americans from June through October of 2015 (source https://fortune.com/2016/07/12/financial-literacy/).

Personal financial plan is a written plan of your own goals, values, current financial state, future financial state, family that you create, income, assets, investments, retirement plan, and a will, which is a legal binding document that tells people in your immediate and extended family and the court what you want to have done (partially divided, equally divided, or percentage division among your loved ones) to your investments, properties, and inheritance after you die.

You should consult a legal professional like an attorney to secure a will for your loved ones. Our advice is to send a copy of your completed will to the court to archive it for you after all legal signatures have been obtained so that in this way no human greed and jealousy can determine the outcome of your inheritance after you die or that any one who alters your will documents after you die will be caught red-handed by the court as not having the original legal binding document.

From retirement planning to credit card debt, college planning to insurance, budgeting to spending, and from saving to even giving, it is always wise to know the numbers that go in and out of your pocket periodically. The good thing is that you don't have to be at a certain age to start your personal financial planning; however, it is rather preferred to start as early as possible.

As a financially conscious person, you need to understand how each of these considerations work together and affect each other, as it is critical to laying the groundwork for a solid financial foundation, not just for you but also for your family.

At a young age when you begin to save money (be it small or large), you will have the freedom to know where to invest your money, and eventually your money will have more time to grow. Our advice is to save money and then invest your savings. Nowadays, having your savings in a saving bank account only yields little to no interest.

Getting to grips with your finances may come off as some unimportant task to you, but little do you know how much it could save you in the long run. Not being financially up to date has caused some families to live in poor conditions and many companies become bankrupt, and being negligent about what you spend your money on and how you spend your money has landed some individuals in a money crisis that they cannot easily get out of.

Another perspective to having a personal financial plan is that it saves you from getting in your own way of destruction and destroying yourself financially. In today's age of information and technology, you can surf the Internet and get lots of wealth and financial advice; however, not every financial advice is sound and good for you.

For a financial plan to make sense, you must first know and accept your current financial reality. Setting your personal financial plan helps you to stay on track, it disciplines your mindset and thinking, and it gives you a feeling of what is important to you and your family and what is not important as in terms of priority. At a certain point in your financially planned life, your priorities and finances become automated as you continue to live your life.

While financial planning may be a tough one to handle, it always pays off in the long run if done correctly. In many advanced countries, most young people are choked with debt because they know little to nothing about personal financial planning. That goes in one way to say that financial wellness is extremely important to our growth and nature as humans, and as you would even notice that large and mid-sized companies now offer financial wellness programs to their employees as part of the onboarding process. To attain financial success, you need to work towards it, bit by bit.

Rewards Point-Based Programs

When it comes to financial planning, we'll advise you to look into your bank's reward programs.

Reward programs are point based programs that banks and financial institutions have for their loyal customers or clients. When you spend money on groceries, restaurants, traveling, friends and family referrals, VIP customers, or even make large deposits, banks or financial institutions make these programs available to engage their loyal customers by giving them benefits and discounts in exchange for their spending activities.

For example, your bank's program might read "buy 3 get 1 for free at a specified place or store". These programs exist for credit card and debit card holders. Since the 2008 financial crisis, some banks or financial institutions have decreased or eliminated their rewards program; however, they do exist. You can even use your point based reward program to book flights for free, sleep in hotels for free, eat for free, or even shop online for free.

Sometimes you may end up sleeping in expansive hotels for free when you travel around the country or world because you took advantage of your bank's rewards point based program. Make sure to get points based rewards for the money you spend from your bank accounts. It is as simple as calling your bank to ask for their rewards point based program and how you could benefit from it. Also, some banks may allow you to transition your current account to a point based rewards account if you never had one already.

How to Invest

The question that we get a lot from the youth and young adults is, "how do I invest?" This is a legitimate question to say the least. We'll recommend to anyone to have an investment schedule because it makes it easier for you and it automates your money into the right places for you to invest. First, you have to create an investment account with a reputable investment firm, schedule recurring deposits (specific dates, weekly, bi-weekly, monthly, or even yearly) from where you have your money saved to go into your investment account.

Regardless of the amount that you want to invest, say you want to invest $50, $100, $150, $200, $250, $300, $350, $400, $450, or even $500 on a specific date within a week, bi-weekly, monthly, or yearly, you would need to schedule money to be automatically withdrawn from the account where you have your money saved to your investment account. This way it saves you from headaches, doubt, and from manually depositing money to your investment account.

Personal Financial Budgeting

Personal financial planning should empower you to do more for yourself. Let's touch a little on budgeting. According to a CNN Money article written by Maurie Backman for the Motley Fool on October 24 2016, "almost 70 percent of Americans don't even have $1,000 in the bank and almost half of Americans claim that to cover a $400 emergency, they would need to borrow the money or sell something quickly to round up the cash" (source https://money.cnn.com/2016/10/24/pf/financial-mistake-budget/index.html).

This is woefully disturbing on many levels. In the same CNN Money article, a study conducted by U.S. banks claims that "only 41% of Americans use a budget even though it's one of the most effective ways to keep track of our finances".

The scary truth is that budgeting is good and effective; however, you don't need a budget to save money if your spending activities are way less than your income threshold. About 59% of Americans do not use a personal budget to plan for their personal finances. The goal should always be to save more and spend less when it comes to personal financial planning. To provide you with more startling information and statistics on financial woe in the United States, we've given you here a source to look at more of the scary financial statistics and to avoid becoming one (https://money.usnews.com/money/personal-finance/saving-budget/articles/2017-05-16/8-scary-financial-statistics-and-how-to-avoid-becoming-one).

50/20/30 Rule- Balanced Money Formula

Now, let's talk about the different approaches to budgeting when it comes to personal financial planning. The 50/20/30 rule is also known as the formula to balance your money by dividing your expenses into three level categorical needs; 50% to needs, 20% to financial goals, and 30% to wants. You can alter the number of percentages to fit your unique situation and conditions such as living in an expensive community, apartment unit, or county or state.

While this budgeting formula is simple, efficient, and flexible, there is a downside to it; that people often find it difficult to identify or differentiate between their needs and wants. The only way to help you by using this budgeting formula is to have your priorities and necessities in mind and categorize your expenses and spending activities.

Zero-Sum- Zero Based Budgeting

Another budgeting technique is the zero-sum also known as the formula for zero-based budgeting by making sure that each month the amount of money leaving your account should be the same as the amount of money entering your account, vice-versa. This budgeting formula helps you to make sure that every dollar or penny in your account has a purpose or job to do.

This technique gives you total control and freedom over your money; however, if you cannot manage or should we say micromanage your personal finances, this budgeting formula can give you unsatisfactory feelings. This formula requires effective time management, attention to details, and immediate and constant tracking of your personal expenditures.

First, you need an Excel spreadsheet, Microsoft Word document, or a budget book to adequately use this formula by creating two columns; in the right column you will need to list your expenses including investments, savings, needs, wants, and any scheduled debt payments, and in the left column you will need to list your monthly income including your second job/income and payments to babysitting or childcare.

Now when you have completed both columns respectively, the right and left columns should cancel each other to ensure that there is a purpose or job for every penny or dollar each month in your account.

Cash-Only Budgeting- The Envelope/File Organizing System

There is another budgeting formula known as the cash-only budgeting also known as the envelope system. This formula to budgeting is unique in such a way that it gives the upper hand to those who like to do things in a visual manner even when it comes to spending.

This formula helps people to become more conscious or sensitive with their spending activities when they use cash for payments instead of credit cards. It gives people the satisfactory feelings of making their finances more accessible or tangible to them. Below we decided to show you how this formula works best.

a. know your net pay or income each month. Net income is the amount you earn after tax subtraction and other deductions from your gross income. Gross income is total pay from your employer before tax subtraction and other deductions.

b. pay yourself first and list your expenses by creating categories such as gas, rent, groceries, investments, savings, etc.

c. look at your bank statements for accuracy on expenditures and decide each month how much you are willing to spend on each expense category.

d. buy envelopes or accordian file organizing folders and write each category of expenditure per envelope or file folder; there should be an investment folder or envelope, savings folder or envelope, etc.

e. go to the ATM machine each month to withdraw money or funds to deposit into the envelopes or file folders.

f.   you should only and always use the cash that you deposit into the envelopes and file folders for their designated budgeting purpose. For example, if your gas money for the month cost $200, you should only take cash from the gas envelope or file folder for the month only. So if you run out of gas money for the month it means that you have used your funds for gas money for the month. It helps you to be disciplined.

g.   when you do have money left over from a month, you have to use that extra money and deposit it into your investment or savings or other ventures that you may have at hand.

h.   now there are some downsides to this formula as well such as constantly going to the ATM machine can be annoying and uninteresting. Only withdraw the amount that you need for a given month in order to avoid having loads of cash on you. Avoid certain ATM machines in order to avoid withdrawal fees from your bank or financial institution. Also you need to consider how a cash-only formula could hurt your credit score since having many spending activities with your card can help your credit score. For that we'll leave it up to each individual or family to use their personal or professional discretion to make a sound decision.

Regardless of the approach to use in your budgeting plans, there will always be benefits and drawbacks among all formulas. However, you need to determine which formula works best for your needs and wants and your family.

Always use your personal and professional discretion to make sound decisions. Whatever doesn't work for you, skip it or avoid it altogether. Remember, don't let your future panic in despair because your present couldn't make good and sound decisions for your future.

"Habits of financial success are learnable, as all habits are, by practice and repetition."
— Shane Johnston

CHAPTER 2
Credit Score

*"If you don't take good care of your credit,
then your credit won't take good care of you."*
-Tyler Gregory

Your credit score is a three digit number (usually between 300 and 850) representation of your creditworthiness expressed in a numerical level of data analysis of your credit report given to lenders by credit bureaus. TransUnion, Equifax, Experian are the most widely used credit agencies in the United States.

We must note to you that there are many different credit scores and models to score you such as custom made models, VantageScore, and FICO. Some lenders and credit agencies use data such as your income when calculating your three digit credit score. It signifies that you have the likelihood to pay back your bills or loans on time.

And the more you have a higher score the more favorable you'll become in the eyes of lenders in terms of creditworthiness. We need credit scores to buy cars, rent properties, lease apartment units, buy houses, apply for business loans, apply for credit cards, employment background checks, etc.

Filing for bankruptcy and having your car repossessed (unable to make payments on your car loan usually stays on your credit for 7 years but it could have dire consequences afterwards on your credit report) can severely negatively impact your credit score.

A chapter 7 bankruptcy will affect your credit score and remain on your credit report for a period of 10 years from the original filing date. A chapter 13 bankruptcy will affect your credit score and remain on your credit report for a period of 7 years from the filing date.

Lenders and creditors will see your bankruptcy filing in the public section of your credit report, and it will significantly be a key indicator of their decision to reject you. Even if your bankruptcy has been discharged and noted on your credit report, lenders and creditors may still have a hard time approving you for certain loans.

Although your credit report will likely not show evictions; however, it could have information on collection accounts for unpaid fees and rent. We must note to you that collection accounts will remain on your credit for a period of 7 years from the missed payment which led to the collection account being open for your unpaid fees and rent.

Usually landlords use a different service to track your rental history such as tenant screening companies or sometimes through Experian RentBureau. Remember that your landlord can file a civil lawsuit against you and win a judgment against you for any unpaid fees or rent.

Your credit reports include your total amount of debt you owe, payment history, percentage of available credit used, the type of debt and when it started, current unpaid debt, new applications for credit, and the length of your established credit history. When you have a higher score it means that you're responsible enough for your credit behaviors either past or present and that lenders and creditors become confident in you to approve you for a loan, credit card, or leasing a property, etc.

Your credit score is an essential part of your financial picture. If you are a borrower, you would know by now that lenders combine your credit score with the information obtainable from your credit report to determine the level of risk involved in the loan process. Should your score turn out to be high, you will have less risk and stand a better chance at getting the loan. But if it is at the downside or very low, nothing is going to stop the lenders from questioning your capacity to pay back what you owe.

Creditworthiness has to do with how you manage your finances in almost every aspect of your life, not just because of the loans, but for your own financial well-being. Your credit score can also significantly affect everything from insurance rates to employment opportunities.

And sometimes many queries to your credit scores within a specified timing can affect it; soft inquiries do not affect your credit scores like checking your own credit scores, a landlord or an employer [although employers won't receive your credit score but your credit history] runs your credit with your approval, and when lenders or creditors run your credit scores to pre-qualify or pre-approve you for an offer, and hard inquiries can affect your credit scores temporarily and appear on your credit report (within few months and up to two years) like when you apply for credit, cellphone accounts, and other certain specified services. The good thing is that some, if not, most credit scoring models do not count hard inquiries into their calculation after 12 months.

A good financial plan is a road that shows us exactly how the choices we make today will affect our tomorrow.
–Alexa Von Tobel

Why It's So Important

A good credit score is like a springboard from upon which you can take flight to your financial freedom and competency. There's so much in store for you when your credit report is filled with the right numbers. In no particular order, here are some of them:

A general look at credit score ranges
- 300-579: Poor
- 580-669: Fair
- 670-739: Good
- 740-799: Very Good
- 800-850: Excellent

Low Credit Card And Loan Interest Rates

Interest rate is one of the costs that you will have to pay for borrowing money. More often than not the interest rate you get is directly tied to your credit score. This happens to be one of the most considered reasons for people to have good credit scores.

If your numbers are just about right, the chances are that you will always be a candidate for the best interest rates. It also means that you will pay lower finance charges on your credit balances and loans. Well, it is worthy of having in mind that the less money that goes into interest, the faster you will be able to pay off the debt.

With a good credit score, you will also be able to have more money to use on other expenses. Even with a good credit score you can apply for financial aid parent grad plus loan for your child to attend college. And if your child has a good credit score he or she can apply for financial aid loans for schooling.

No Security Deposits

Having a good credit score will help you side-step security deposits in utilities. Such fees can fall between $100 and $200, depending on the region of the country, and it can be a strong clog in the pipeline of your relocation plans. Well, you may not have it in mind to change residence any time soon, but you always have to plan ahead for rainy days and part of the planning is to make sure that your credit score is looking right and good.

In such a case, a credible credit score would mean that you will not have to go through the stress of paying a security deposit when you establish utility service in your name or when you transfer service to another location.

Access To Higher Limits

As you may already know, your borrowing power is pretty much contingent upon your level of income and the numbers on your credit score. If you are creditworthy enough, banks will be more willing to allow you to borrow large sums of money than you could if your score is low, because you will have shown to the institution that you always pay your debts fully and on time.

It is essential to say that a bad credit score may still be able to land you a loan, but in such a case, the amount borrowed will be limited to what the bank feels you will be able to repay. Just as the saying goes: to whom much is given, much is also expected. Your credit score is the one thing that says it all.

Easy Rent Approvals

Great credit scores make approvals for rental houses and apartments more hitch-free. The real estate market is now at a stage where a proliferating number of landlords are basing their tenant assessments on credit scores. This means that during these screening processes, having a bad score may make the lessor raise an eyebrow and even hesitate to rent out a property to you.

If your bad credit happens to be the aftermath of a previous eviction or yet-owed rental balance, it can seriously ruin your chances of moving into a new apartment. If your report is good enough, it will save you a fortune in time and squabble as per finding a landlord that will approve your rent.

Negotiation Power

If you want to negotiate on a lower interest rate negotiation on your credit card or a fresh loan, getting a good credit score is the way to go. Are you in need of more bargaining power? You can take advantage of other attractive offers that you have obtained from other firms based on your credit score.

If your credit score looks awful, creditors may balk at budging on loan terms, and you will not have other credit offers or options. Now, do you see why having your credit report nice and polished helps you have bragging rights out there?

Although not all creditors report to the three widely used credit agencies, TransUnion, Equifax, and Experian; however, lenders and creditors may use a blended score of your credit from the three credit agencies. Some creditors even report to only one or two or all three.

Drive What You Want

*Modern man drives a mortgaged car over a
bond-financed highway on credit-card gas.
-Earl Wilson*

Unless you are financially capable enough to buy the car of your dreams, chances are that you will have to secure a loan to ride one. And, as with all other kinds of loans, your credit score had better be smiling or else you will get kicked out of that lender's lobby.

Your score does not only affect whether you will qualify for the loan or not but also the amount of interest that you will have to pay on the loan.

In general, loan applicants with good credit will always have the upper hand in larger amounts and lower rates, enabling them to get the needed money to purchase a vehicle. It is also important to know that a higher interest rate means you will contend with a higher car note each month.

Getting A Job

As the world is changing, many more employers see the need to conduct credit checks as part of the HR process. While most of them check credit reports rather than credit scores, it still narrows down to your financial responsibility, as that will make the prospective employer either hesitant or willing to bring you on board.

In some cases, the employer may decide to let you go upon finding that your level of debt is too high for the salary to be offered. Some of these organizations go as far as updating themselves on your credit score before giving you a promotion or a salary raise, especially for executive and financially-related positions. Employers may see your credit history but not your credit score.

Starting A Business

With a well-written business plan, perseverance, curiosity, and persistence, you can secure a loan to start your business. It is virtually a dream to most people to start a business. Even if you have a seven-digit salary, an inner ambition can still push you to invest in an enterprise, which is most commonly called "business entrepreneurship". When starting a business you must consider alternative lending options available to you.

For those who may not have the luxury of cash, they will turn to a bank or any other financial institution to acquire a loan. And for that application to go through, you need to have a good credit score report on your credit sheet. While there are many other factors at play, obtaining that small business loan would be something that your credit score will facilitate. If you want to become a business tycoon someday, your finances need to be as clean and efficient as possible, right from the very start.

If you have a bad credit score and report, you may want to try alternative options like small business microloan and other lending options discussed below. Also, as you decide to start your business, you may not have an established business credit report or business tax filing documents; however, lenders and creditors may rely on your personal financial statements, tax returns files, and your personal credit score and report.

If you want to start your business or if you have an already established business, you can begin to monitor your FICO SBSS Credit Score. This monitoring helps you to gauge what lenders or creditors look at when applying for business financing. Checking your FICO SBSS credit score won't be able to hurt your credit scores.

Another tip is to sign up for a free consulting account with agencies to help you monitor your FICO SBSS credit score, and when you do sign up with agencies they give your business free 24/7 hours access to monitor your business scores and reports. Some agencies may allow you to have a free account, but may require a recurring monthly fee to have premium level of access to other things in your account. Find out the terms and conditions before signing up with your business.

To get small business loans for your business you need to have an effective business plan with well-thought marketing strategies detailing your growth and business forecast on future costs and cash flow, and determine how much funding that you need as a business entity. Check your personal credit scores with all three major credit bureaus before applying because your lenders and creditors will do their own work and obtain your credit score and report. Obtain records of your personal and business IRS tax documents, and anyone who is involved with your business as a stakeholder must have their tax documents ready.

You will need relevant legal contracts that you have signed on behalf of your business such as business incorporation, franchise documents, any property leasing documents, etc. And make available any personal financial statements or documents including credit cards, accounts receivable, investment details, unpaid invoices due to you, etc.

Remember that you as a business owner need to ask yourself some of the honest and tough questions such as how much is too much funding?, how much can I afford in a monthly payment?, etc. And as a business owner you need to look at things from the lenders or creditors perspectives such as how risky is the type of business that I am doing?, what is my credit score and report?, do I have the expertise and experience to do this type of business?, if I fail as a business owner how can I liquidate my assets and to whom?, how quickly will my business prosper or become profitable?, and is it worth it to pursue this venture after all?

You can use some of your retirement funds to fund your new business start-up costs even though it is not the most advisable thing to do. You can use your ROBS plan, 401(k), or IRS savings to borrow funds from your retirement savings to fund your new business; however, it is not a wise decision to withdraw funds from your retirement savings to fund your new business venture as starting and running a business comes with many intolerable risk.

If your business model is to work with equipment or heavy machines, there are equipment financing loans available as well as equipment leasing options, and if you would like to get a credit card for your business, there are business credit card loans available as well. If you default on your equipment financing loans, your lender or bank can seize your equipment as collateral to pay or cover the cost of their lost money. If you prefer to go the route of small business administration SBA loan, there are options available to choose from.

Remember that the Small Business Administration SBA office guarantees loans, but it does not make loans. Lenders and creditors go through the strict standards of the SBA office and become approved through the SBA loan programs to make loans available to small business owners and small businesses.

Let's look at the different types of SBA loan programs; the popular ones that most business owners and businesses go for:

SBA 7(a) loan program offers business loans up to $5 million U.S. dollars. According to the 2020 fiscal year report, about 17% of the SBA 7(a) loan program money went to small business start-ups. This type of loan favors those with vast experiences in their specified industry such as an experienced physician opening his/her own private practice or those who prefer to buy a franchise or an already existing business that has been established for years. To qualify for $350,000 U.S. dollars or less with this type of loan program, the SBA office requires you to have a minimum 155 range FICO SBSS credit score in order to avoid having a manual credit review.

Remember that the FICO SBSS is considered a commercial credit score ranging from 0 – 300, and it combines your personal credit score report and that of your business partners or co-owners as well as the business credit of your business entity.

SBA Express loan program offers loans up to $350,000 U.S. dollars to small businesses. This type of loan program helps to speed up the processes to get an SBA loan faster since getting an SBA loan isn't easy or fast. To qualify, you need a good or acceptable credit score and report; however, there is no minimum credit score required to apply.

SBA 504 loan program offers loan to businesses and business owners who are looking to purchase real estate and larger equipment.

SBA Export loan program offers loan to businesses and business owners who participates in international trading.

SBA Microloans program offers a term loan with 72 months as the maximum and 40 months as the average loan term to businesses and business owners to fund their business capital, supplies or inventory purchases, fixtures, machines, equipment, and furniture. The maximum loan amount under this program is $50,000 U.S. dollars and

$14,000 U.S. dollars as the average loan offer. This type of loan is given to businesses and business owners by Community Development Financial Institutions and other Non-Profit organizations that serve as intermediaries for the SBA office.

Let's look at other microloan lenders that work with community development financial institutions to give loans to businesses and business owners:

The Accion Loan program is flexible when it comes to credit requirements and assistance to help applicants. The Accion loan program works with their community development financial institutions to make loans available in the amount of $300 U.S. dollars to $250,000 U.S. dollars.

The Kiva loan program is a community-based trust-driven platform for businesses and business owners. This loan program has a 0% APR financing to struggling entrepreneurs who are unable to have access to other pertinent financial funding, have a business that has strong social impact, who can invite their own networks of lenders, and have proven their character through acceptable means and beyond a reasonable doubt. This loan program helps businesses and business owners to crowdfund business loans from individuals with philanthropic-mindset up to $15,000 U.S. dollars.

KickStarter and Indiegogo are rewards platform that allow entrepreneurs and those with a vision to raise money for their business venture or business project(s).

The Role of Debt and Equity in Starting a Business

There are many ways to fund your business; however, it depends on the value of debt and equity. When you decide to go the route of debt, investors receive legal binding documents detailing obligations such as interest, repayment, timing, and other terms and conditions for his or her cash.

Albeit, you maintain complete ownership of your company; however, you are obligated to your investor and signed legal documents to terms and conditions, and if you do not meet the obligations your investor could force your company to go into liquidation (the process of bringing a business to a close end or distributing its parts to shareholders or claimants).

When you decide to go the route of equity, you are not obligated to pay investors because you decided to give a percentage of ownership stake of your company to an investor in return for the investor's money. The reality check is that you will not have full control of your own company and that you'll have to make important decisions with your investors.

Not all debts are bad debts. You can use debt to fund your business ventures by going for small business lenders. Use Google and other search engines to search for small business loan lenders. Some organizations are willing to lend their money to small business owners.

Remember that these small business loan lenders will give you a short term loan within 30 days and the interest rate can be high. Go for Small Business Administration SBA loans because they help small business owners to secure loans from more established financial institutions; however, you are required to pay the loan back. Go for loans at established financial institutions. These financial institutions require you to have assets and a business plan and EIN number ready in order to secure the loans for your business.

As far as equity is concerned, there are several ways to look for funding from investors such as:

Angel Investors (affluent individuals who form investment groups to mitigate risk in businesses. To find such people you need to visit your local chamber of commerce because they will have an idea of who is interested to fund new business ideas in your community and or search online for angel investors in your community or nearby cities).

Venture Capital Firms (they want to take a controlling percentage of interest in your company by making large investment money available during the early stage of starting your business).

Self-funding (basically using your 9-5 job to save enough to fund your business is one of the best ways to start a business or applying for credit cards or selling something of value to generate enough money to start your business).

Partnership Alliance (having a strategic partnership can help your business venture with monetary resources and sharing other resources available).

Crowdfunding (helps individuals with business ideas to reach out to web and media platforms to many like minded people or supporters. Some platforms can be rewards [KickStarter and Indiegogo], equity [Wefunder], or debt [Kiva] based platforms. It is important to do your research before approaching this method).

Family and Friends (this can be either debt or equity depending on the nature of the terms and conditions involved. You can even sell a percentage of your business to family and friends, but you have to be extremely careful as losing funds due to investment or market trends can cause your loved ones to feel betrayed, hurt, and bitterness at your family events or personal meeting spaces. First you need to know the risk involved and educate your family and friends on your business venture before deciding on anything).

Invoice Financing (it helps to avoid cash flow issues during invoice cycles. It simply means that you get paid by your clients or customers through invoices. This can be different from doing invoice factoring measures. This option requires less paperwork involved and you can get your money or financing as little as in a day).

Bootstrapping (using your business money or personal assets to fund your business venture with no help from anyone. At this point you have decided to go alone).

"Pay off your debt first. Freedom from debt is worth more than any amount you can earn."
–Mark Cuban

CHAPTER 3
What You Should Know About Debt

*"Debt is like any other trap, easy enough to
get into, but hard enough to get out of."*
-Henry Wheeler Shaw

Unless you're one of the few born with a silver spoon, you would know that debt is a critical part of almost everyone's life. Whether it is running up a credit bill during an online shopping spree or borrowing a couple of thousands of dollars, living with the feeling that you owe someone or some people money is something you will have to handle at some stage in life.

But the bad thing about debt is that when it gets out of control, as that can place you under some serious financial problems and even emotional predicaments. Ultimately, more and more debt will bring about results that could literally give you sleepless nights.

Own Your Assets

Did you take out a mortgage for the home in which you currently live with your family? If yes, then it's the bank that owns the home, not you. The same thing applies to your car and auto loan - not yours. But when you make it a lifelong practice to always be debt-free, you will stand a better chance at owning more assets such as the property you live on, the car you drive and even the clothes you wear.

And, owning these things means that you don't have to live with the worry that someone can knock someday to take your belongings, all because you were unable to pay up what you owe. Managing and clearing debt, literally, helps you become and stay your own boss, answerable to no one but yourself.

More Free Income

When you accumulate too much debt, the payment on such debt swallows a huge fraction of your income. For example, if you have a 30-year mortgage for $200,000 at an interest rate of 4.5 percent, the payments on your mortgage will consume $1,013 of your income each and every month.

That also means that almost half of that amount will go into interest, which does not build any kind of equity on the property. But if you can figure a way to be punctual about paying that debt, you will have over $1,000 of extra income for yourself every month.

If anything, that is more than $12,000 every year, just about enough money you can spend on anything that matters to you, from kitchen remodeling to investing in something to going on a vacation every year. In every way, having more free income comes with a good feeling much better than owing someone.

Financial Security

"The SECRET to financial security is not to have more money, but having MORE CONTROL over the money we presently have."
-Auliq-Ice

It is something most people do not know, that debt is a real menace to your financial security. Above all else, debt prevents you from making the most of your money. The money you spend on debt payments could form a great stash for a day you will be in the most need of it. It could go into your retirement days or for the college expenses for your kids.

In the same way, the money you constantly send out to cover debts could be used as an investment, an anchor upon which you could make more money to handle other things in your life.

The main point is rather than allowing yourself to be ridden by debt; you can be conscious about your personal finance and save money for unforeseen circumstances. Once you attain that debt-free status, you will then be able to work towards becoming a more financially secure individual.

Earlier Retirement

The trouble with retirement is
that you never get a day off.
–Abe Lemons

If you are wondering about the things you could do with the money you have saved up, you can put it into investments. If you are doing a bad job at putting sufficient money into your retirement accounts as from now, those extra bucks could make all the difference. It will determine whether you will hand in your boots at 65 or still have to go to work in your golden years.

If you are already working on your personal retirement contributions through your employer, you can still reach financial security by investing in a lucrative business. It will help you to stop working earlier in life, and allow you to be financially comfortable while in retirement rather than depending on your grand kids to survive in your old age.

Mental Health

*"Every time you borrow money,
you're robbing your future self."
-Nathan W. Morris*

Becoming a debt--free individual has more benefits, as it can also help you achieve wellness of the mind. According to a research study by Northwestern University, people with too much debt are 13 percent more likely than average to have symptoms of depression (https:// news.northwestern.edu/stories/2013/08/high-debt-could-be-hazardous-to-your-health).

Let's look at this one, per information obtainable from a 2014 study published in the Journals of Gerontology: Series B, effects similar to depression are found in adults over 50 years of age (https://academic.oup.com/psych-socgerontology/article/69/5/763/2940062).

Having many debts that are not backed by assets have a strong link to mood swings, and the symptoms get worse when the amount of debt is higher. On the extreme side, debt can lead to suicidal tendencies; an article co-edited by Barbara Ehrenreich and Gary Rivlin has been cited by a 2012 Huffington Post report which says that people struggling with student loan debt often battle with suicidal thoughts, and a few have fallen prey to it (https://www.huffpost.com/entry/student-loan-debt-suicides_b_1638972). Further, a debt-free person has more improved mental health, as he or she is less likely to be anxious or depressed.

Better Self-Esteem

"The worst loneliness is to not be comfortable with yourself."
–Mark Twain

When you owe people too much money, it can have a stain on your self-esteem. Many psychologists and debt experts have concluded that people with debt are more likely to create a life that looks great on the outside, possibly with a nice house, girlfriends, cars, and flashy clothes. They may do a good job at concealing their debts and making people think they are at the top of the money chain. Because all these things cost money, they could be in an unbearable degree of financial predicament, which could increase their feelings of shame. On the flip side, paying off debts can boost your self-confidence and morale.

In some stories, people say that they are motivated to buy a new car when they pay off their debts. Knowing that your credit check would come out fine gives you every reason to hold your shoulder high, touting that you are truly independent and financially secure.

Better Credit Score

As we have discussed, your credit score is the main thing that talks about your financial habits on paper. When you carry lots of debt, it can drag down your credit rating. And, the closer your credit cards and loans are to the limit, your score is not going anywhere high.

A bad credit score can cost you thousands of dollars a year in higher interest rates, which makes it even harder to break free from a current debt problem. A financially wise individual who knows better than to stack his debts until they come crumbling will improve his credit score, which in turn, comes with its own benefits such as lower insurance premiums, better job prospects, more attractive deals on cell phone service, better interest rates and many others. In the long run, the numbers on your credit report tell the story.

Your credit score doesn't measure wealth or success, it measures your relationship with debt
-Anonymous

CHAPTER 4
Retirement Hacks

"Investing is not nearly as difficult as it looks.
Successful investing involves doing a few things
right and avoiding serious mistakes."
–John Bogle

Acritical aspect of your personal financial life is how well you fare during your retirement years. Not waiting to be old before investing is an ideal thought to be considered as well as saving for your future should be one of the priorities on your personal financial planning list.

Sadly, there are many people who do not put it in mind, and never mind putting it into practice. Thanks to the Employee Benefits Research Institute, we know that at least 24 percent of workers and their spouses have less than $1,000 in savings for their retirement.

Almost half have less than $25,000, which shows that a scary number of us are in need of a reality check concerning how much we save and need to save for retirement. Well, the good news is that it is not over until it is over. It is never too late to start saving more and spend less, and there are a plethora of hacks to help you make it.

Real Estate

> *"Real estate is an imperishable asset, ever increasing in value. It is the most solid security that human ingenuity has devised. It is the basis of all security and about the only indestructible security."*
> *–Russell Sage*

Real estate is considered one of the ways that people can plan a successful retirement. When done correctly, investing in properties can help you make money now and continue to make increasing amounts for the rest of your life. Contrary to what many people might think, you don't need to be wealthy to own an apartment complex. You can just start off with a small, single unit rental and take it up a notch from there.

Depending on where you live, every state has areas where rent is more than the average price of a mortgage. All you need to do is to find such an environment in your state and start looking for the best opportunities. Securing funding for real estate investing is also considerably easier than most people know, since there are many methods one can use to get cheap or affordable real estate properties at nearly no cost to themselves.

When you are able to find the right home, consult with a licensed and experienced real estate agent to know more of the options to take to become a real estate owner and how it can benefit you financially in the long-term. Think about other options such as using your house or apartment unit to do Airbnb or a private hotel in your community. Having a group of close friends with each chipping in $5,000 or $10,000 can help in the pursuit of real estate to buy properties and rent it out to make extra money for retirement savings.

Think about forming legitimate partnerships with strong alliances to take other approaches in real estate development such as wholesaling; when a wholesaler contracts a home with a seller and then finds an interested party to buy it at a higher price than what the seller would usually sell the house for. The wholesaler then keeps the difference as profit margin.

Recently, did you hear that the National Association of Realtors (NAR) wants to ban wholesaling entirely?

This wholesaling business has become a long battle between licensed real estate agents, government officials, and wholesalers. The government wants to tax wholesalers who earn big profit margin from selling properties, and licensed real estate agents feel that it is unfair to real estate professionals to have people who are unlicensed and unregulated with no code of ethics to make contract deals and make fortune out of it.

We agree that there are uneducated, untrained, and predatory wholesalers out there who cause more harm to homeowners than good. And states requiring licensure will be the key to reduce unhealthy competition and unwanted predatory behaviors in the real estate marketplace. Some wholesalers will sell a house worth $30,000 to buyers for $80,000 and keep the difference without disclosing it to the property owner(s).

Policy Analysis: Real Estate laws are regulated at the state level. Each state should pass "predatory wholesaling laws" just like Oklahoma, North Carolina, Illinois, and Pennsylvania did. In the case of North Carolina, a wholesaler must fully disclose the assignment fee they make as profit margin to the seller. In Illinois, wholesalers must have a broker's license and be subject to the Illinois Department of Financial and Professional Regulation; there's a $25,000 fine per violation in failing to meet the rules & regulations. In Oklahoma, any contract dealing with a wholesaler without a real estate license is illegal.

In Philadelphia, PA, wholesalers must have real estate license, and failing to have a license will result in violations and penalties, and the seller has the right to nullify sales with any unlicensed wholesaler including where sales' disclosures are not fully disclosed to the seller.

Recommendations: New state rules and regulations will present challenges and barriers for wholesalers and investors. However, change is needed to protect homeowners from predatory behaviors and people. New regulations must bring awareness to homeowners as well as educate them to make the best decision for their families and property. Look for your state's rules and regulations on wholesaling in the real estate marketplace.

Watch Your Spending

Do not save what is left after spending;
spend what is left after saving.
—Warren Buffett

Keeping in mind how much goes into what you spend does not mean you have to sacrifice all of your modern conveniences. It also does not mean you have to penny pinch so tightly that you can hardly buy yourself a cup of coffee. It means keeping expenses low as well as tracking your monthly financial obligations and making sure they are in check.

One of the costly mistakes people make in this aspect of personal financial planning is that they start spending immediately after they start earning from a business. You need to know the limits and threshold of your budgeting, and make sure to pay attention to special details in your financial planning. Outrageously spending habits now will cost your retirement planning and future.

We are not suggesting to you to starve yourself; at all times, be comfortable and live happily with yourself. To have a better future plan, you need to be aware of how you spend and put more effort into not buying things you do not need.

Eliminate Mortgage For Instant Rise

"The universe of mortgage lending has gotten to the point where there is a place in it for everyone."
–Joe Mays

For a lot of people, living expenses stand in the way of retirement goals. Here's something you may not know: since your biggest expense is perhaps your mortgage, the best way is to pay off your mortgage loan and get rid of it for good.

One of the easy ways you can get yourself a raise in retirement is to make that house totally yours. You can make extra payments and whittle at it bit by bit. But remember not to dismiss the idea of selling your home and downsizing to one which you can simply pay for in cash, because that will instantly free up thousands of dollars that could go into building your nest egg.

If your monthly mortgage is $1,200, for 12 months that is $14,400 in annual cash flow. To come up with that amount, you must financially plan for your life and future. So if you are paying off the mortgage or downsizing, you will save money to plan for retirement. And if you invest that money, you could have enough saved to fund your retirement for years to come.

Start A Venture

*"Why start a second job, when you can
start your first business."*
–Wendy Gavin

If you want to retire early and be well off, you may want to consider starting a business that will become your cash flow. If it beats your imagination, then let it sink in that there are many people out there who earn substantial amounts of money annually just by committing to a business idea.

For instance, someone could just buy fabric at a discount in China, sell it to people in the United States via a platform like Amazon and keep the difference in their pocket. While this may not be the most interesting of ideas, it can completely be automated to make you a lot of bucks.

The good news is that there are plenty of free online tutorials that teach people how to make money through online e-commerce -easily and lucratively. All you need to pull this off is some motivation, with which you will set a plan and get to know the specifics. Apart from making moves to help secure your years of retirement, you can start a business to become accomplished, create a sense of financial discipline and learn how to be effective at managing almost anything.

Relocating

You can have your way into living a less expensive life to make the most of your retirement savings. You should opt to live in affordable communities if that becomes an option to you. If you have a seven-digit salary, nothing should be bothering you. But if you earn less and want to retire on a limited income, you may want to change your location. There are many methods that you can use to save, and a few of them include cutting down on your spending, taxes by living in affordable communities, gas prices, housing and even groceries.

When you move to a tax-advantaged state, province, or region in your country, you can save thousands of dollars in any given year. Some states in the United States require no state income tax and some states do. An efficient financial planning enables people to pay off their mortgages and real estate in just a handful of years, making the rest of their income totally free and available for investment opportunities for retirement.

Lower Earned Income And Maximize Passive Income

"Never depend on a single income. Make an investment to create a second source."
−Warren Buffet

If you have lived in the United States for long enough, you would know that earned income is taxed even with the recent tax changes in the country. Come to think of it, there are federal, state, city, and payroll taxes. Meanwhile, passive income is taxed to nothing, so shifting your income from earned to passive can help you to reduce your tax bill.

Even if your single source of income is from a W-2 job, you can still set up your portfolio to become tax-free. Furthermore, the tax planning decisions you make in the future should be in alignment with your new goal of being taxed at the least rate possible. Creating genuine passive income is kind of the holy grail of personal financial planning.

Remember that not all passive incomes are created equal, because some streams take much more initial effort to start, probably requiring you to save enough to buy your first rental property. But once started, it doesn't take a herculean effort to gain traction. When you retire you will need to be financially secure; this is not up for debate. You can take matters into your own hands rather than having to depend on someone for your financial freedom.

CHAPTER 5
Becoming a 401(k) Millionaire

"Every day is a bank account, and time is our currency. No one is rich, no one is poor, and we have got 24 hours each."
-Christopher Rice

No one should work for 30 years to 60 years only to save $1,000 for retirement, but you can do well by changing your strategies now and make it possible to triple the size of your investment account. Your success depends on how much you learn and how much you invest.

A 401(k) account is typically a retirement savings plan under the auspices of an employer, one which helps workers save and invest a portion of their salary before taxes are deducted. In this initiative, taxes are not paid until the money is withdrawn from the employee's account. If you have a 401(k) or something similar, the wisest thing you can do is to learn about retirement investing and maximize the long-term growth power of this provision.

Regularly Rebalance Investments

*"You must gain control over your money or
the lack of it will forever control you."
-Dave Ramsey*

While the initial step in planning your 401(k) is asset allocation, it is just as important to re-balance your investments as time goes on. This is critical due to the fact that one asset may outperform another, especially if stocks happen to do better than bonds, making your portfolio disproportionate.

Re-balancing your investments can also be a move in the right direction as you gradually get older and need to shift some assets away from high risk such as stocks and turn them into lower-risk ventures such as bonds. The main idea behind this is not letting your 401(k) capacity dwindle away with ups and downs, because as time goes on you need to establish a new equilibrium to keep the cash flowing and safe.

Consider Lower-Fee Investments

"Investing should be more like watching paint dry or watching grass grow. If you want excitement, take $800 and go to Las Vegas."
-Paul Samuelson

It is a common misconception that it costs nothing to invest in a 401(k). Contrary, this never happens, not even if you are free of direct fee charges. The investment options for your 401(k) include mutual funds, which naturally charge their own management and administrative fees. Known collectively as the expense ratio, it is expressed as a percentage of the fund's assets.

For instance, a 1 percent expense ratio implies that of every $100 you invest, $1 will go into paying fees every year. The investment ratios mandated by your investment options are always available in the narrative of your plan. It is also a great idea to compare fees charged by your funds, just to find out if there is a chance that there would be lower-cost options that accomplish the same investment objectives.

Know Your Company's Vesting Plan

"If you fail to plan, you are planning to fail."
–Sir Winston Churchill

Many companies out there have a vesting schedule to match 401(k) plans. The fact is the money does not really become the employee's until they have been with the company for a specified amount of time. If you tend to change jobs from time to time, you need to be aware of the specified time period from your employer.

In general, out of every four jobs, one does not have a full vestment, hence forfeited money. One out of every two millennial forfeits their 401(k) when they change jobs. This means that when you hop between jobs, it can substantially reduce your retirement income when you retire. So, it is important to know the vesting plan of any company you work for in order to come to grips with when it is best to change jobs for the good of your 401(k).

Stay Put With Stocks During Market Crashes

"Buy when everyone else is selling and hold until everyone else is buying. That's not just a catchy slogan. It's the very essence of successful investing."
–J. Paul Getty

One of the ways you can make the most of your 401(k) is to stop yourself from pulling out of stocks when there is a market crash. Some people cannot bear the sight of their stocks remaining in the market when they are plummeting down. Just because there are a few shifts doesn't mean you should pull it all out, because this is one of the worst decisions you can make for your long-term retirement strategy.

There is no denying that market crashes can really frighten people and could lead to split-second decisions. Nonetheless, if anything, that is actually the right time to buy stocks rather than selling the ones you already have. A lot of research has shown that the average investor significantly under-performed in the market over time. A huge reason for this is the emotional, knee-jerk reactions to market fluctuations. Look on the bright side and stay put.

Leave The Money In The Account

There is often the temptation to withdraw some money from your retirement account to attend to petty expenses. But, as much as you can, just leave the money in the account until you are finally retired. This is not about taking early cash-out distributions from the account- you should never even do that by the way. 401(k) loans may come off as a great idea initially because the approval process is easy, the interest rates are low, and you're going to pay yourself back with interest.

What most people are unaware of is a well-allocated portfolio of stock and bond investments can be expected to return some 7 percent each year on average. So when you borrow money at 4 percent rate; for example, you will be robbing yourself of some of the ROIs that could eventually turn your 401(k) into a huge retirement nest egg.

Increasing Your Contribution Rate

According to suggestions from experts, you should plan to allocate no less than 10 percent of your monthly income into your 401(k), excluding your employer contributions. To some people, this can sound like a lot from their paycheck, but you should bear in mind that you do not have to get there all too immediately.

Of the many 401(k) strategies, it has been found that most people are more okay with starting with the exact amount that their employers are willing to match. After doing this, you should increase your contribution rate by 1 percent every year until you are putting 10 percent of your income into that account, or what your ultimate target is. By doing this, you will hardly notice any difference, but it can really help you with the growth of your retirement savings. If you are among the ones that want to grow their nest eggs as much as they can, then this is one way to do so.

Have An Emergency Fund

To a considerable extent, just about everyone should have an emergency fund. The question that is likely to pop up here is: how exactly is this said emergency fund related to retirement savings? Well, when you are in need of some quick cash, you can dip into your 401(k) and take small amounts of money. But, if this happens too often, you may end up having no savings at all.

So, it is essential to start up an emergency fund, even if you put in about $10 to $20 every seven days. For example, if your water heater or air conditioning unit develops a fault, you will have some funds to repair rather than tapping into your retirement savings.

The best way to start an emergency fund is to work with your current financial institution and begin a direct deposit into your savings account or to another checking account. Do make sure this is a savings account or another account from your personal ones and think of it like an old vacation club or Christmas club accounts banks once offered.

CHAPTER 6
The Right Way to Invest

"To acquire money requires valor;
to keep money requires prudence;
and to spend money well is an art."
–Berthold Auerbach

Many people do not buy the idea of investing because they believe you that you need a lot of money to start, say thousands of dollars. No, you can start investing with as little as $50 a month, and just like that, you are on your way to making extra cash with your extra cash. Make it a plan to save up some money from your income or use your end-of-year bonus to contribute toward your personal financial planning.

And you need to know about the right and efficient way to invest in order to double and triple the money. The master key to building wealth is developing good financial habits such as regularly putting money away in savings every month. If you make investing a habit now, you will become financially stronger in the long run.

Compound interest is the eighth wonder of the world; he who understands it, earns it; he who doesn't, pays it...
-Albert Einstein

Entrust Your Money To A Robo Advisor

If you do not have the required skills to invest on your own and not enough time to brush up on them, you can hire a robo-advisor, especially if you are not so willing to loan your money out to some people you do not know online. Robo-advisors are more or fewer investment companies that pride themselves in creating automated software designed to manage portfolios following certain guidelines.

When signing up with them, you can take a questionnaire to determine the rate at which you can tolerate risk and find out your investment goals. It is their job to make investment management possible for the masses since they ordinarily have low account minimums - sometimes even nonexistent. Some of these advisors offer state-of-the-art user interfaces to help you monitor your investment performance, holdings and much more all in a snapshot.

Peer-To-Peer Lending

Perhaps the whole idea of online trading does not suit you well. Then, there's a chance you will like the option of investing in the lives and ideas of others and earn some interest. Just as exciting as it is reasonable, peer-to-peer lending involves loaning money to people through an online service whose focus is to bring borrowers and lenders together.

When you give out some amount of money for a borrower to maybe pursue a business, you will expect it to return with some interest. If you invest in a platform such as Lending Club, you can do so automatically by using their lending criteria.

Alternatively, you can manually invest by browsing available loans and selecting the ones you like. Like any other investment, peer-to-peer lending is such that you can make sure to choose the path that suits your tolerance for risk. Thankfully, Lending Club helps you know which pathways are less risky than others.

Look Into Your Employer's Retirement Plan

Should your budget be very tight, even the most basic step of enrolling in your 401(k) or employer retirement package may seem far fetched. But you can invest in an employer-sponsored retirement plan with a very small amount, such as 1 percent of your salary. You may not miss a contribution so small, but the tax deduction you will get for doing so will make it easier and the contribution even smaller. After that 1 percent, you can increase gradually every year.

When you time the increments with your annual pay raise, you will notice the increased contribution even less. So, getting a 2 percent pay increase will effectively be split into your retirement plan and your checking account. If your employer provides a matching contribution, it will make the entire arrangement even better.

Mutual Funds

Mutual funds are investment securities that allow you to put your money into a portfolio of stocks and bonds with a single transaction, making them usually perfect for newbie investors. The likely hassle is that many mutual fund companies demand initial minimum investments ranging from $500 to $5,000.

For a first-time investor who has just a little sum to put in, the minimums can be out of reach. But the good news is that some of these companies can waive the account minimums for you, only if you give the nod to invest every month with $50 to $100 automatically.

Automatic investment is quite common with mutual funds and ETF IRA accounts. Even though it is less common with taxable accounts, the question is whether it is always available to you. Also, automatic investing is specifically convenient if you can do it through payroll savings.

Treasury Securities

There is an insignificant number of small investors who start their investment journey with U.S. Treasury securities. But that does not mean it is a bad idea. As much as you can never get rich investing this way, it is yet a safe and excellent place to save your money and earn interest until you are ready to make your inroad into more tangible investment options. Also known as savings bonds, treasury securities are easy to purchase via the U.S. Treasury's bond portal Treasury Direct.

That is where you can get some fixed-income U.S. government securities with maturities ranging from 30 days to 30 years in $100 denominations. You can also make use of Treasury Direct to buy Treasury Inflation Protected Securities (TIPS). They do not just pay interest, but also make periodic principal modifications to account for inflation.

Real Estate

You should know first that not everyone is cut out to be a landlord. Rather than running too fast to buy an investment property and risk losing to imbalances, you need to be efficient enough to consider other options. There are many ways to invest in real estate without having to deal with physical properties because sometimes going all in may teach some hard lessons you will never forget. While there is no one saying you should go cash-for-house when all things are equal, you can as well consider investing in real estate notes.

Someone can buy a pool of properties the right way, and people like you would invest money into the owner's project. From there on, he or she will manage the homes and pay you a dividend or interest off that money. If you don't want to go through the stress of being a lessor or dealing with sometimes stubborn tenants, this is an attractive way to make money easily.

Diversify Your Money

In this business if you're good, you're right six times out of ten. You're never going to be right nine times out of ten.
–Peter Lynch

Financial advisors often point out that not diversifying money is one of the worst mistakes people can make. Even if it is just $1,000 you have to spare in the long run, make sure to diversify it. With ETFs, it doesn't cost a fortune to diversify your money and to make sure you're not riding a single-stock roller-coaster. On the other hand, you can buy some shares in a company with that $1,000, but that move will not be setting you up for making smart investment decisions in the future.

Even if you think it is just some change, you need to be smart with your money and start practicing now for the future. Build your portfolio over time and do well to re-balance it as certain investments within the portfolio can fluctuate in value. Do not simplify or over-simplify in any area, but learn to diversify your portfolio.

"The best thing money can buy is
financial freedom."
–Rob Berger

CHAPTER 7
ETF and Stock Trading Basics

"Rule number one: Don't lose money.
Rule number two: Don't forget rule number one."
-Warren Buffett

When a company completes an Initial Public Offering (IPO), its shares become publicly traded on a stock market, which are venues where buyers and sellers of shares meet and decide on a price to trade. These secondary markets are where existing owners of shares can have transactions with potential buyers. It is essential to understand that the corporations listed on the stock markets don't buy their own shares regularly.

As for exchange-traded funds (ETFs), they are ideal for newbie investors because of the numerous benefits such as low expense ratios, abundant liquidity, an extensive range of choices, the option to diversify, and a low investment threshold among others. If you are looking to invest in any of these two opportunities, here are some basics you should have covered.

"Everyone has the brainpower to make money in stocks. Not everyone has the stomach."
–Peter Lynch

Stock Trading Basics

- Because millions of investors are on the stock market with opposing views, it is an adversarial system you should be well-versed in before venturing.
- As numerous factors determine the rise and fall of stocks, a certain type of sentiment is created, where more sellers than buyers lead to a fall and more buyers than sellers make the stock prices rise.
- The stock market is not predictable, so you need to understand the point at which stock prices are fairly valued, the event that will lead to a tumble and the human decision-making processes to buying or selling shares.
- The real price of a stock is factored by market activity, so when looking to buy or sell, it is often wise to compare a stock's actual price to its fair value.
- The best time to buy is when others are overly pessimistic in the market, and the best time to sell is when the same others are overly optimistic.

• Some stock markets rely on professional traders to maintain continuous bids and offers because a motivated buyer and seller may not be able to find each other at a given moment.

ETF Trading Basics

• Technically, an ETF works a bit differently than a mutual fund does. Mutual funds essentially buy and sell securities for cash on the open market; the process for an ETF is more complex.

• ETF attributes such as diversification and tight bid/ask spreads make them well suited for swing trading, and a beginner can choose to trade sector-based ETFs because they are available for different investment classes.

• Individual investors can add ETFs to their portfolio by buying them via a broker just as they would when they are purchasing stocks.

• ETFs can be traded throughout the day from open market to close market, and they allow investors to diversify their holdings within a group of securities.

• When you trade in and out of an ETF, you will incur a cost that can make them less suited to systematic investment programs like dollar cost averaging while reducing any cost efficiencies.

Solomon Oppong and Felix O. Quayson

"Unless you can watch your stock holding decline by 50% without becoming panic stricken, you should not be in the stock market."
–Warren Buffett

Conclusion

Whether you are just entering college, fresh out of graduation, or looking for a new job in the labor market, the time to start perfecting your personal financial planning is now. Do everything within your power to stay out of money trouble and become a financially liberated person.

We kindly ask you to use your personal and professional discretion to make sound and safe decisions. Above all, get in the mood to take your personal financial planning very seriously. The consequences are intolerable if you refuse to plan for your financial well-being and future.

Always believe in yourself that you matter the most. And do not treat yourself like you are an option. You're the consequential image of yourself. And if you have created a family, there's more for you to do financial planning, and to be on the right track with your family and loved ones.

Do not become miserable in life because you did not have the knowledge to be financially literate. Now, you have no excuses because you have this book and other books to educate you on the fundamental basics of personal financial planning in order to continue to your journey of becoming financially literate and free.

Do not discount yourself and your ability to do and achieve greater things in life. We believe in you that you can do everything that you set your mind to achieve. Your mindset matters the most in your path to personal financial planning and freedom.

As we have discussed, living debt-free and planning your life rids you of all the worry that comes with owing people and not having enough money to take care of your own basic needs. From what you buy to the way you invest, you need to be conscious, effective, efficient, and smart about your financial decisions in order to live a life free of financial problems.

Remember the Rules of financial freedom:

"Rule number one: Don't lose money.
Rule number two: Don't forget rule number one."
-Warren Buffett

ACRONYM TERMS AND MEANING

ETF – Exchanged Traded Fund
IRA - Individual Retirement Account
401(k) – Retirement Savings & Investment Plan
SBA - Small Business Administration

JOURNEY TO FINANCIAL LITERACY AND FREEDOM

Solomon Oppong & Felix Oppong Quayson

To our families, friends, and readers!!!

Thank you!
We believe in You!!!

ABOUT THE AUTHORS

Solomon Oppong, MBA
(Purdue University, Western Governors University,
& Cornell University Graduate)

SOLOMON OPPONG is a Ghanaian-American Financial Expert and Real Estate Agent residing in Fort Worth, Texas USA. He emigrated to the United States in his twenties as an international student in search of financial freedom with only $200 dollars in his pocket and had no family to help him. Solomon decided to read one personal financial book every month. With his hardship and hard work, Solomon figured a way to put himself through college, become credit card debt free, and started investing with the little money he had saved. Today, Solomon is a multi-million dollar real estate agent producer and investor, and shares his vast financial knowledge to people from all over the world and teaches people about personal financial freedom. He is married to Doris, a Registered Nurse Practitioner, and they have two sons, Josiah and Jeremy. His goal is to help people to gain and understand financial literacy and freedom. He is a graduate of Purdue University (Bachelor's degree), Western Governors University (MBA degree), and Cornell University (Commercial Real Estate Development). Solomon Oppong can be reached via email at solomon7365@gmail.com

ABOUT THE AUTHORS

Dr. Felix Oppong Quayson

DR. QUAYSON has worked in diverse professional roles in health care, higher education, and state and local government programs, serving as a graduate school professor, researcher, author, international research editor, reviewer, college board of trustee, board of directors member, founding editor-in-chief, founder of employment respecialization training program, medical liaison, data analytics specialist, performance, measurement, and quality improvement specialist, document control manager, training manager, disaster case manager, emergency immigrant outreach worker, chaperone for year one medical scholar pipeline program, mental health volunteer, independent health specialist contractor, and founder and chief executive officer of Quaysearch Health Inc. In 2010, he received an award in the pursuit of wellness at Greenspring Erickson Retirement Community in Springfield, Virginia. Dr. Quayson's research interest is in Education (including policy studies, EdTech, STEM, adult ed, leadership, teacher ed, higher ed, multicultural, and entrepreneurship), Research Methods, and Workforce Development. Specifically, his scholarly work focuses on understanding Performance Metrics Outcomes, Career Pathways, Students Readiness for Employment and Transition to Workplace, and the Symmetrical Relationship between Workforce Development and Career Technical Education- particularly for marginalized students of diverse ethnic and racial backgrounds. Currently, he's a Researcher on a U.S. National Science Foundation (NSF) grant award in STEM. You can reach Dr. Quayson via email at dr.felixoquayson@gmail.com

Also Available from J. Kenkade Publishing

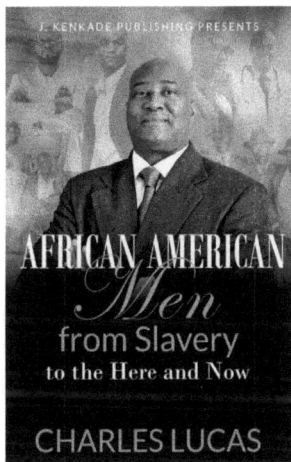

ISBN: 978-1-944486-74-7
Visit www.amazon.com
Author: Charles Lucas

An overview of great African American Men and how they have fared as leaders from the brutality of slavery to where we are today after the election of the first African American President of the United States of America. The author focuses on leaders in areas such as the educational field, the religious sector, corporate America, the United States military, and in the United States government. Very little time is spent on the achievements of African American men. Therefore, the author believes that our sons and daughters need a short, comprehensible walk through the past that may be shared with peers of all races so that they will know what it took to get us to the here and now.

Also Available from
J. Kenkade Publishing

J. KENKADE PUBLISHING PRESENTS

THE *Face* OF
THE *New*
ENGINEER

Dr. Lashun K. Massey

ISBN: 978-1-944486-66-2
Visit www.amazon.com
Author: Dr. Lashun K. Massey

The autobiography provides an account of the life of Dr. Lashun King Massey, P.E. It outlines the challenges that she faced growing up as a child in rural Arkansas. Although Dr. Massey was born in a socioeconomically depressed area in Arkansas, she managed to defy the odds and pursue a career in engineering. This book helps shed on light Dr. Massey's childhood and uncover the challenges that she faced in pursuing a career in engineering.

Also Available from J. Kenkade Publishing

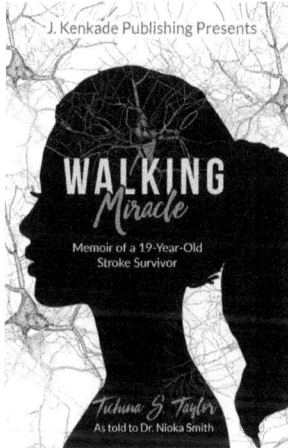

J. Kenkade Publishing Presents

WALKING Miracle

Memoir of a 19-Year-Old Stroke Survivor

Tichina S. Taylor
As told to Dr. Nioka Smith

ISBN: 978-1-944486-68-6
Visit www.amazon.com
Author: Tichina Taylor

A major stroke interrupted her life at the tender age of 19, when life was just beginning for her. Find out how this stroke survivor fought against the attack on her own brain to defeat the odds within her physical, spiritual, emotional, and even her academic life.

Also Available from J. Kenkade Publishing

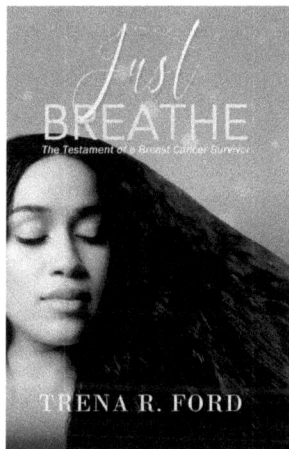

ISBN: 978-1-944486-98-3
Visit www.amazon.com
Author: Trena Ford

"Just Breathe" is the true story of a small-town girl born in the Delta. The youngest girl of five children, Trena Ford's life was changed radically when her family relocated to follow an evangelical church ministry. Throughout her childhood and into her mature years, she had a special bond with her father that granted her opportunities to experience triumphs as well as heartbreaks. She tells the story of how a cancer diagnosis, devastation, and death uncovered an unshakeable seed of faith buried deep within her soul. Through pain and several medical procedures, she was given a formula that birthed new life into her desire to overcome cancer, live on purpose, and fulfill God's plan for what He created her to be.

www.ingramcontent.com/pod-product-compliance
Lightning Source LLC
Chambersburg PA
CBHW071111210326
41519CB00020B/6258